World

The

MW00893700

Published by G-L-R (Great Little Read)

Written by Keith Goodman

This book has been written for children aged seven and over, and it is part of the English Reading Tree Series.

Your child will be able to read the majority of words, but those that cause difficulty should be read together and pronounced slowly.

This is the perfect tool for parents to get their children into the habit of reading and focusing them on how words are formulated and used within simple sentences.

If a word does cause difficulties, make sure to re-read the sentence containing it, again, and go through the meaning if necessary.

Here is a fun activity before you start to read

How many things do you know about WW1?

1   What year did WW1 start?

2   What month did Britain declare war on Germany?

3   The soldiers of which country were called Doughboys?

4   What year did America enter the war?

5   Which was the biggest battle of the war?

6   Why did the Russians ask for peace?

7   Where was the peace treaty signed

8   What happened at Scapa Flow?

Table of Contents

The Road to War

The start of World War 1 was caused by a combination of factors that had been building up for years.

This was a time of great change on the continent of Europe and the great powers such as Britain, Austria-Hungary, Italy, France, Russia, and Germany had many an old score to settle.

The mixture of political intrigue, imperialism, and national interests created a very unstable situation at the start of the twentieth century, which was mixed with secret alliances and mistrust.

It only needed a spark to send these countries spinning into war, and that spark came with the assassination of Archduke Ferdinand of Austria.

Friends and Enemies

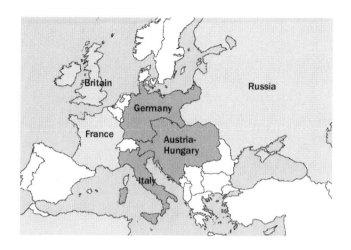

Germany had an alliance with Austria-Hungary and Italy from 1881. These countries made a pact to help each other if any one of them was attacked by France. The Italians, however, made a secret alliance with the French, saying that they would remain neutral.

In direct opposition to the alliance between Germany and Austria-Hungary, the French and the Russians became allies in 1892.

In 1907, the famous Triple Entente (alliance) was created between Britain, Russia, and France.

Germany felt threatened by the triple alliance as it was now surrounded and could be attacked on two sides.

The Great Empires

France and Britain had built up vast empires around the world and because of this were incredibly wealthy and powerful. Both Germany and Russia were envious and wanted to do the same. This race to colonize the third world would lead to some bitter conflicts.

The Path to War

Archduke Franz Ferdinand who was heir to the throne of Austria-Hungary was assassinated in Sarajevo (Bosnia) on June 28, 1914.

Austria believed Serbia was to blame and declared war on July 28, 1914.

Russia was the ally of Serbia and began to mobilize its army to help fight Austria-Hungary.

The ally of Austria-Hungary was Germany, and it declared war on Russia in August 1914. Several days later, Germany also declared war on Russia's Triple Alliance partner, France and sent troops to invade Belgium.

Britain, as part of the Triple Alliance, then declares war on Germany on August 4, 1914 for invading Belgium.

The First World War had begun.

Trivia

At the start of the war, the USA was neutral and hoping to stay that way.

The German plan was to conquer France quickly so that it could then concentrate on Russia.

At the beginning of the war, all of the countries involved thought that it would be over by Christmas.

Out of all of the European countries, it was Britain that had the biggest empire. This included large parts of Africa, the Middle East. Canada, Australia, and India.

Meet the Two Sides

Fighting a war is a bit like having an argument with somebody and then involving your friends. At the beginning of the First World War, there were two very distinct sides. The Central Powers consisted of Germany, Austria-Hungary, Bulgaria and the vast and powerful Ottoman Empire. The Allied Powers were Britain, Russia, and France. The USA entered later.

The Central Powers

The Leaders: Kaiser Wilhelm the Second (Germany), Emperor Franz Josef (Austria- Hungary), Sultan Mehmed V (The Ottoman Empire) and Tsar Ferdinand (Bulgaria).

The Kaiser

Germany had a massive army and was generally thought of as the leader of the alliance. The German commanders used the Schlieffen Plan, which was an attack strategy based on fighting a war on two fronts. The aim was to overrun France and subdue Britain first. It would be then possible to turn the attention to Russia. Unfortunately, for Germany, the war didn't go according to plan.

The Allies

The Leaders: Georges Clemenceau (France), David Lloyd George (Britain), Tsar Nicolas the Second (Russia), and Woodrow Wilson (USA).

 Lloyd George

Even though the chain of events that started the war was caused by Russia defending Serbia against Austria- Hungary, the Russian Revolution in 1917 meant that they made peace with Germany.

Trivia

Although Belgium had declared itself neutral; Germany still invaded and brought Britain into the war.

The Central Powers put together a vast army of more than 25 million troops. Of this number, more than eight million were wounded and over three million killed in action.

The allies had an army of around 42 million troops and auxiliaries. During the period of fighting, almost 13 million were wounded and six million killed. Russia and France alone suffered catastrophic losses.

America's Part in World War One

Because there was a percentage of US citizens who had emigrated from Germany, the US wanted to stay neutral and not pick sides. However, some events occurred, which changed the mind of Woodrow Wilson, the president. The entry of America into the war had a significant effect in favor of Britain and France. Without the US the war could have stayed locked in a stalemate for many more years.

So why did the US enter the war?

Even though the sinking of the passenger liner the R M S Lusitania altered the public opinion of Americans, it wasn't the decisive event. A German U-Boat torpedoed the Lusitania off the coast of Ireland on May 7, 1915. There were 1,198 deaths, which included over 100 Americans.

The infamous Zimmerman telegram was the last straw that helped send America into the war. A high-ranking German Official, Arthur Zimmerman sent a message to his ambassador in Mexico. He wanted the Mexican government to become Germany's ally if America entered the war. He offered help to get back land that had been taken from Mexico by the US.

The British intercepted and decoded the message in January 1917. America declared war in April.

Even though the build-up of American troops was slow, by the time the war ended, there were just over two million American soldiers in Europe. This gave the allies a big boost and brought down the moral of the Central Powers who were losing the will to continue the fight.

Trivia

It is estimated that 116, 000 Americans lost their lives in the war, with 322,000 wounded.

The US troops were called the American Expeditionary Force, and the soldiers were nicknamed 'doughboys.'

One of the biggest mistakes that the German Command did in the war was to admit that the Zimmerman telegram was authentic and had not been faked by British intelligence as a means to bring

America into the war. Once America had sided with the Allies the end result was inevitable.

US troops in France, marching to the frontline

Apart from soldiers, the American Navy blockaded German ports and made them run short of war materials and food.

Trench Warfare

The fighting in the First World War involved opposing armies digging trenches as a way of defending themselves. These trenches would carry on for miles and miles and were protected by machine guns and barbed wire. It was difficult for either side to make any progress.

The fighting in France and Belgium was called the Western Front, and the trenches stretched from the North Sea through Belgium and France.

Because of the trenches, neither the Allies nor the Central Powers made much progress for nearly four years. From October 1914 to March 1918.

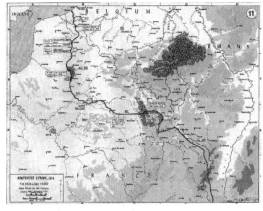 Western Front

How the trenches were built

It's hard to imagine life in this period. Mechanical diggers didn't exist, and the trenches were dug using manpower. Soldiers used shovels and picks. The ground that was in between the two opposing trenches was called 'No-Man's-Land.' The enemy trenches could be as close as just 50 yards or as far away as 250 yards.

Conditions in the Trenches

 Life in the trenches

It was normal for a trench to be around twelve feet deep and protected at the top with barbed wire. Most trenches also had sandbags at the top for extra protection and the mounting of machine guns. The bottom of the trenches had wooden boards.

There were front line trenches, and support trenches and these were connected by trench paths to allow the soldiers to move around.

Trenches during the First World War were disgusting places to spend time in. There were rats and lice and all sorts of diseases, including Trench Fever and Trench Foot. Sanitation was very basic, and the food was revolting.

Trivia

It is thought that the total length of trenches built during this war would be over 25,000 miles.

Trenches were always in need of repair as they were attacked not only by enemy shells but also the extreme weather.

This was still a very primitive form of warfare and soldiers would use their guns like spears when they attacked the opposing trench.

Most of the attacks across No Man's Land took place very early in the morning. An attack was called 'Going over the Top." Meaning leaving the trench.

The Major Battles of World War One

The Battle of Marne (1st)

It is true to say that at the beginning of the War, nobody knew how long it would eventually last or the way that the method of fighting would quickly become bogged down by trench warfare. The Germans wanted a very quick offensive on the Western Front, and there was some initial success. However, the German advance soon ran out of momentum due to long supply lines and lack of manpower. They were forced to retreat at the Battle of Marne on the 6-10 September 1914.

One of the lessons learned at Marne was how lethal modern weapons were in open fighting. After Marne, both sides began to dig trenches to protect themselves.

The Gallipoli Campaign

French heavy gun firing at Gallipoli

The extent of the incompetence on the part of allied leaders was never more on display than at the landings in Gallipoli. The idea of the attack was to eliminate Turkey from the war and allow shipping to pass through the Dardanelles, which was the 60-mile space of water separating Asia from Europe. The Allied leaders thought the Turkish troops could be overcome very easily, but they were wrong.

Allied solidiers landed on the Gallipoli peninsula in Turkey on the 25 April 1915. Fierce fighting occurred, and the allied forces were stopped by the Turks. Trenches were dug and in the heat of summer sickness and disease was as much of a killer as Turkish bullets.

The allies eventually retreated and finally left the peninsula on January 9, 1916.

The Naval Battle of Jutland

Damaged German Battlecruiser after Jutland

On May 31 until June 1, 1916, the British and German fleets fought it out at the Battle of Jutland.

Once again, the British were able to break the German code and intercepted a message about an ambush of their ships in the North Sea.

The ships that did battle were huge iron monsters called Dreadnoughts.

The action involved two hundred and fifty ships.

Neither side gained control, but the German's retreated. This meant that the British ships kept control of the vital sea routes, maintaining their naval dominance.

In fact, Germany lost only 11 ships in the battle to Britain's 14.

The Battle of Verdun

This was the longest battle of the war and lasted from February 21 until December 18, 1916. This was a hard fought encounter with many German and French lives lost.

More than 400,000 German troops were killed in this battle and around 550,000 French.

Because of the number of French troops killed, it was left to British forces to lead the 'Big Push' that was being planned to end the war.

The Brusilov Russian Offensive

One of Germany's big miscalculations was about the Russian Army. It was thought that by the time, it had been mobilized; the fighting on the Western Front would be over. This would have enabled German troops to go to the Eastern Front (Russian Front)

The initial German campaign against Russia had been successful, but between June 4 and September 20, 1916, the Russians would begin to fight back. The offensive took its name from the Russian military commander Aleksei Brusilov.

The tactics used by the Russians were so successful that they were used on the Western Front. Artillery fire at the beginning of the attack helped weaken the defenses before the troops charged the enemy lines. Even though the offensive was a complete success, it would be the last before the Russian Revolution.

The Battle of Ypres (Passchendaele)

The Battle of Ypres started in July 1917 and continued until November. It is also known by the name of the village it was fought around, Passchendaele. The region where the battle took place was of high strategic value to both sides. The Passchendaele ridge was eventually captured by Canadian troops on November 10, but like many battles during the war, it was not a decisive victory for either side. Both armies suffered huge numbers of casualties during the campaign.

The German spring offensives

This was the last chance for the Germans, as they attempted to break through the British lines in 1918. The advance started in March and continued through July. Even though there was some success by the German troops, the British line was pushed back but never broken. In the end, the Germans paid an enormous price in soldiers being killed and injured, without that much ground taken. By July, the Germans had been stopped, and the British went on the offensive.

The Battle of Amiens

The Battle of Amiens lasted from August 8 until August 11, 1918. It was the start of what has come to be known as the hundred day's campaign, which came directly after the German spring offensive. From this moment onwards, the allies were steadily advancing and pushing the Central Powers back.

This battle came towards the end of the war, and the allies had learned a lot about tactics. They used troops, airplanes, and tanks to push the Germans back. The British Expeditionary Force (BEF) advanced over seven miles on the first day of the battle using these tactics.

Ultimately the plan of the allies to make small gains and then hold on to them against counter attacks, paid off. Towards the end of 1918, the Germans were staring defeat in the face.

The Battle of Megiddo

This fighting took place between the 19th and 25th of September 1918 in Palestine, which is in the Middle East. This was a decisive Allied victory against the Ottoman Empire, and one of a number of battles that forced them to withdraw from the conflict.

The great empires of the world were crumbling and the Ottoman Empire was no exception. The alliance with Germany would mark the end of this empire and the emergence in 1923 of modern day

Turkey, under the leadership of Mustafa Kemal Atatürk.

Armored car at the battle of Megiddo

The Battle of the Somme

This battle was the biggest of WW1 and gets its name from the river near where it was fought.

The battle commenced on July 1, 1916, and lasted until November 18, 1916.

The troops at the Somme consisted of the British and French on one side, and the Germans on the other.

The leaders of the allies were Douglas Haig and Ferdinand Foch. The German army was led by the three generals, Rupprecht, von Gallwitz and von Below.

As was often the case during WW1, the leadership on both sides left a lot to be desired.

The battle started with an allied bombardment of the German lines. This was designed to destroy them.

However, even after the eight days of constant bombing, the Germans had suffered very little damage.

Military intelligence told the leaders this, but they were not believed, and the attack went ahead.

German troops at the Somme

On July 1, the British attacked the German trenches and were met by a sea of bullets. The first day of the Somme was one of the bleakest days in British military history. There were 60,000 wounded and killed. However, the attacks continued, and by November, the deaths and casualties had risen to around 623,000 British and French soldiers.

The Germans had also sustained around half a million deaths and casualties.

The Battle of the Somme was one of the bloodiest in the history of the world.

Trivia

This battle saw the use of tanks by the British for the first time.

The Allies gained around seven miles by the end of the battle.

The campaign ended because of atrocious weather conditions.

The Use of Tanks in WW1

British Mark 1 tank at the Somme

Tanks were highly unreliable and very slow moving in the First World War. The Tank was a British invention and could be used very effectively to break through the barbed wire so that troops could get across No Man's Land.

Compared to the modern day tank they were extremely slow and could do a maximum of four miles an hour. They were also unreliable and broke down easily.

The conditions inside a WW1 tank were cramped, smelly and dangerous. The Germans destroyed most of the Allied tanks during the conflict. Germany was not convinced of the effectiveness of these machines and because of this build only a handful.

By the last year of WW1, the British and French had constructed 6,500 tanks, but when the war eventually finished, the British only had eight left.

Tanks were to come into their own in the Second World War but between 1914 and 1918, were still a 'work in progress.'

The War in the Air

German Fokker

Eindecker

It had been only a comparatively short time at the beginning of the WW1 since airplanes had been invented. After many disastrous attempts, it was the Wright Brothers in 1903 that created the blueprint of the planes that flew in this war.

The real problem in 1914 was how to use planes in warfare. The military on both sides saw that having superiority in the air was important, and by 1918, the air force had become a vital part of military strategy.

The obvious use of planes during WW1 was to look at the position of the enemy and the movement of enemy soldiers. This was called reconnaissance. The planes became the eyes of the army.

The early bombers of the First World War were primitive and could be shot down easily. As the war progressed, the planes became quicker and could carry bigger bombs. Even at the end of the war, though, they were still not that effective. The warplane would come into its own during WW2.

It was inevitable with so many planes in the air above the battlefield that they would start to fight each other. The planes had machine guns. The gun was synchronized with the propeller to allow it to fire without damaging it.

Fights between planes were called 'dogfights,' and some of the pilots became famous because of their skill. The most famous of all was a German who was nicknamed the 'Red Baron.' Other pilots, who were considered good, were called 'Aces.'

The planes

Bristol 22: This was a two-seater British fighter plane.

Fokker Eindecker was a German warplane designed for one pilot only.

Siemens-Schuckert: a German single-seater fighter.

Sopwith Camel: This was a single-seat British fighter.

As well as planes, there were floating airships that were flown during WW1. The Germans used airships to bomb Britain during the war.

Trivia

The German airships were called Zeppelins

The fastest that a WW1 plane could travel was about 100 miles an hour

Military markings of each country were important to stop planes being shot down by troops on their own side.

Zeppelin Raid on London (1915)

Zeppelin in Flight

A Zeppelin airship attacked London on May 31, 1915. This was the first time that London had ever been attacked from the air. Even though Zeppelins could not do that much damage with their bombs, they scared the population.

The Kaiser didn't want there to be a raid on London because he was very close to the English Royal Family. He eventually gave the order for the attack but didn't want bombs to destroy the history of the British capital.

Zeppelins had gondolas that were suspended underneath the rigid frames. These gondolas contained the engines and bombs.

The huge airship arrived in London just after 11 pm and bombs were dropped on the East End of the city.

The Zeppelin was so high up in the night sky that the British defensive guns could not see it.

Even though the raid was a complete success, the British got revenge and destroyed the Zeppelin while it was docked in its home base in Belgium.

The Christmas Ceasefire

One of the strangest events that took place during the war happened at the end of 1914. There was an unofficial ceasefire between the two opposing armies because of Christmas.

The ceasefire wasn't official, so in some places along the Western Front, the fighting continued.

British and German troops meet in 'No Man's Land.'

It was the Germans who started the truce by lighting candles in their trenches and singing Christmas carols. The British and French began to do the same. In the end, some soldiers from both sides met in 'No Man's Land,' and actually exchanged gifts. There were also some troops that played soccer against each other.

The Red Baron

The Red Baron sitting in his airplane

The most famous World War 1 pilot was a German who was nicknamed the Red Baron. His real name was Manfred von Richthofen. The British pilots called Richthofen the Red Baron because of the color of his warplane.

Richthofen was a member of the German elite fighter squadron that was led by Oswald Boelcke. He shot down his first Allied plane in 1916 on September the 17th. He was soon the most decorated pilot in the German Air Force.

In 1917, he painted his plane red and was promoted to a commander of what was called the 'Flying Circus.' This was a group of the best German pilots.

The Red Baron was the top fighter pilot of the war and shot down 80 enemy planes. He was shot down and killed in July 1917.

The Russian Revolution

There was a revolution in Russia against Tsar Nicholas II. The Revolution meant that the Bolsheviks gained power and a new country was created by the now communist government that was called the Soviet Union.

The war with Germany and its allies had caused huge discontent in Russia from 1914. The Russian Army was massive but poorly equipped and badly trained. A staggering two million Russians were killed in battles during WW1, and five million were wounded.

The Red Revolutionary Army

After the revolution had occurred, the Russians made peace with Germany and exited the war.

This gave a boost in the short term to the Germans because they could now just fight on the Western Front. However, any boost was short-lived, as the Americans entering the War, was a massive blow.

The End of the War

With the tide of war flowing in their favor, the Allies decided to go for a big push to force the Central Powers to surrender. The Hundred Day Offensive started in August 1918 and drove the Germans out of France.

The Germans retreated to Germany and called for an armistice. This is an pact where both sides agree to stop fighting. The Allies agreed, and the war finally came to an end at 11 am on November 11, 1918.

Whether the Allies should have invaded Germany and forced surrender rather than an armistice has been argued about for many years.

The Treaty of Versailles was signed in 1919. It was an extremely tough treaty and forced the Germans to pay money for the damage caused by the war. The Germans also had to give up land and totally disarm. Many saw the Treaty as a huge victory for the Allies, but others saw it as a recipe for disaster.

The Germans never forgave the Allies for the Treaty of Versailles, and it would ultimately lead to the Second World War.

 Allied leaders at Versailles

There were some significant changes to the face of Europe after WW1, and a number of new countries were created. These were Czechoslovakia, Yugoslavia, Finland and Poland. The Ottoman Empire turned into Turkey, and Alsace-Lorraine moved from being German to French.

The League of Nations was created, which was an attempt to maintain peace on the planet. There were 42 founding members.

Trivia

The USA was not one of the signatories of the Treaty of Versailles. America made its own peace with Germany.

The USA did not become a member of the League of Nations.

The money that Germany owed the French was never fully paid back.

The Tragedy at Scapa Flow

Under the strict conditions of the armistice, the German fleet sailed to Scapa Flow in Scotland to await their fate. While it was being discussed what to do, Admiral Ludwig von Reuter who was in command, gave the order to scuttle the ships. This meant that the German Navy sank its own ships.

SMS Bayern slowly sinking

The reason why Germany did this was to stop the allies dividing the ships out amongst themselves. The sinking took place on June 21, 1919.

A Glossary of WW1

Allies: A treaty between France, Russia, Britain, Italy and Japan. The USA was an 'Associated' country but never part of the core alliance.

Armistice: When both sides agree to stop fighting each other it is called an Armistice, or truce.

Artillery: These were very large guns that were used to bombard the enemy lines.

Blockade: This was done to stop supplies and armaments arriving or leaving an enemy country.

Central Powers: These were the countries that fought against the Allies. They were Germany, Austria-Hungary, The Ottoman Empire and Bulgaria.

Christmas Truce: A cease-fire at the front between the armies. This was never recognized officially.

Doughboys: American soldiers were called this nickname during WW1.

Dreadnought: The Dreadnought was a huge heavily armed battleship that was at the height of its power during WW1.

Eastern Front: This was the war being fought in Eastern Europe. The Central Powers were up against Russia and Romania. The Russian Revolution forced a truce.

Front Line: The front line is where enemy armies fought each other.

Kaiser: This was the name that was given to the German Emperor.

League of Nations: A group consisting of 42 countries created after WW1 to promote world peace.

Lusitania: this was a luxury passenger liner that was torpedoed by a German U-Boat off the coast of Ireland. More than 1000 passengers were killed.

No Man's Land: This is defined as the area between the two enemy trenches.

Prussia: This was a region in the German Empire. It included Poland and parts of Northern Germany.

Schlieffen Plan: The Germans wanted to beat the French quickly so that they could concentrate on attacking Russia.

Treaty of Brest-Litovsk: The peace treaty that ended the war between Russia and the Central Powers.

Treaty of Versailles: A harsh treaty that was signed to end the hostilities of war.

Trench Warfare: This is warfare where both sides dig defenses into the ground for their protection.

Triple Alliance: An Alliance between France, Britain, and Russia to defend each other against attack.

U-Boat: This is what German submarines were called.

Western Front: This is the region in Western Europe were fighting took place between The Central Powers and France, Britain and the USA.

Zimmerman Telegram: Was the message that eventually brought the USA into the war on the side of the Allies. Germany wanted a pact with Mexico against America.

How much did you learn about WW1?

1   What year did WW1 start?

2   What month did Britain declare war on Germany?

3   The soldiers of which country were called Doughboys?

4   What year did America enter the war?

5   Which was the biggest battle of the war?

6   Why did the Russians ask for peace?

7   Where was the peace treaty signed

8   What happened at Scapa Flow?

Thank You for Reading this Book

You can visit the English Reading Tree Page by visiting:

Visit Amazon's Keith Goodman Page

Books in the English Reading Tree Series by Keith Goodman include:

1 The Titanic for Kids

2 Shark Facts for Kids

3 Solar System Facts for Kids

4 Dinosaur Facts for Kids

5 American Facts and Trivia for Kids

6 Christmas Facts and Trivia for Kids

7 Space Race Facts for Kids

8 My Titanic Adventure for Kids

9 Save the Titanic for Kids

10 Halloween Facts and Trivia for Kids

11 Discovering Ancient Egypt for Kids

12 Native American Culture for Kids

13 Meet the Presidents for Kids

14 The Universe and Stuff for Kids

Made in the USA
Columbia, SC
16 April 2019